Redeemed

A World of Disillusion Book 3

Brandalyn Hollen

A Live For 'It' Series

To Mrs. Ochs and Ms. Semino. You were the teachers that made all the difference.

To My Father

Your journey ended far too early. I know death was a whole new adventure for you, and you are always looking down on us, watching over us. I love you Dad.

This is a work of fiction. Any names, characters, businesses, places, events or incidents named in this book are for fictitious effect only. Any resemblance to actual persons, living or dead, or actual events is purely coincidental.

Chapter Guide

Chapter 1 Warmth

Chapter 2 Reconnecting

Chapter 3 Abandoned

Chapter 4 Revival

Chapter 5 The Rescue

Escaping

"We cannot escape what we cannot control"

The day arrived quickly. To the small band of travelers there was no end in sight from the long mountain pass. The map showed nothing but long expansive mountains. Stopping, sleeping, eating, going, stopping, sleeping, eating, going, there seemed to be no end in sight. The group was irritable and began to lose faith in this unknown destiny. As they moved along a midday storm trapped the four travelers in the passage. They were unable to move backwards, for the snow made the upward passage going back too difficult; they could not move forwards because the fog and snow was blowing straight in their faces.

Dileon and Loeric were able to cut one of the tents open and make a makeshift lean-to against the mountain walls. It was little shelter, but it did allow them to get a fire going and stay somewhat warm. Anna took stock of their rations; they were down to only a few strips of dried meat. If they did not catch any fresh meat soon; they could all die. Huddled together the storm raged on, and the travelers stayed trapped in the hazardous mountain passage.

****

Doctor White entered the room and was surprised to see the young girl passed out against her stepfather's arm. "Poor thing! She must be so tired. It can be difficult on some of the patients to adjust to the routine. We believe in keeping the teenagers busy to avoid any negative behaviors."

"She was starting to yawn and be sleepy and then the next thing I know she's passed out snoring on my arm." Rick laughed as if this was nothing new.

Liz hadn't even been in the bathroom for ten minutes and came back to Anna passed out too. She had noticed her getting sleepier before she left the room. It was really nothing new for Anna to pass out where she slept. Liz remembered when Anna was fourteen and they had visited her old school friend. Anna had fallen asleep on

Liz's lap on the front porch. Anna was not a heavy child; she was tall but still very thin. Liz often worried her weight was not healthy; then she would see Anna eat and realize the child had a very fast metabolism. "Are we free to take her home now?"

"Yes. Yes of course! I just need you to sign a few papers and then we can get you out the door. I have one of the staff gathering her belongings, including her shoes and coat; I know its cold out there."

"Thank you." Liz hurriedly looked through the paperwork and signed everywhere she seen the highlighted line.

"If you are interested, at no cost to you, we have drug testing services. You can bring Anna down anytime. The lab is good about getting the results back instantly. The center also provides supportive individual counseling and family counseling. I would strongly recommend counseling for the family."

Liz was feeling uncomfortable. She needed to get out of this place. She definitely was not interested in counseling. It would probably do her and Anna good, but they had their own way of dealing with their issues.

"Thank you. I will take a look at the information. When do you normally work so if I have any questions, I could call you?" Liz knew what the doctor wanted to hear and wanted to seem as parental as possible.

The mother was not fooling the doctor. Doctor White felt something was off about this situation. She would normally recommend a longer stay for children such as Anna. Her initial evaluation showed the doctor Anna was either very self-destructive, or someone else was hurting her. The doctor suspected someone else was hurting her. The mother had a slightly yellow bruise showing through her foundation. The problem was she could not prove any abuse and had no legal grounds to hold the teenager.

Doctor White put on her best face, "I am usually here in the afternoons until about nine pm. Here is my card which includes my work cell number; you can call or leave me a message anytime!"

"Thank you again." Liz handed the paperwork back to the doctor. "Wake up Anna! It's time to go home." At first, Anna barely stirred. Then Rick began to move, and Anna shot straight up.

"What?"

"Time to go home sleepy head." Liz had a clearly, noticeable nervous giggle.

"Oh. Okay."

The small 'family' of three left the doctor's office and headed to the main desk to pick up Anna's few belongings. Anna could barely see but she still managed to get her shoes on. The coat was draped around her shoulders. She felt so warm already. *I do not know what the son of a bitch gave me... I can barely walk! He is so stupid he would drug me in a rehabilitation center. Apparently so.*

Anna struggled to keep her eyes open as Rick helped guide her to the familiar little Ford car. Liz walked to the car and entered the passenger side. Anna laid down in the back seat. The seat was not very long across but worked enough for Anna to go to sleep. Rick and Liz were going to surprise Anna with the new trailer house. Liz decided she would still live at Todd's house; as everything seemed to be going well. Rick and Liz had worked hard to set up a very nice room for Anna. It even had a corner desk for her room. Liz had made sure Anna had clean clothes and clean bedding. She knew how much Anna hated dirty laundry.

Anna was so tired she could not comprehend where they were at. It all looked a blur to her. She allowed her mother to guide her into the room and she laid her down on a comfy, familiar bed. It felt like ages since she had laid down with her own blankets. She felt even if they weren't her blankets, they were still fresh, clean and so very comfortable. Liz went back into the living room and sat down on the black futon. "I think I am going to crash here tonight, and then I will make Anna some breakfast. Do you think she will like that?"

"Ya. That would be nice. Liz, you can stay as long as you want to!"

"Tonight, is long enough. I will need to get back to the house after breakfast, before Todd gets home from work."

****

The storm raged through the night and the next day. The youth were hungry. All the rations had run out. Even the horns filled with water had ran out. Anna and Zoey were able to use a stew pot to collect snow and melt it over their small fire. It was not large enough to melt the snow instantly, but after a while the snow had melted enough for everyone to have a decent drink. Anna continued to use any magic she could without success. Her faith was dwindling. *Where are the gods now that I need them more than ever!* During the night when all was dark except the small glow of the fire, Zoey broke down into a hysterical fit. "This is where we die! I saw us all from a distance, covered in snow, dead!"

Anna tried to calm her sister the best she could, but Zoey would not have it. She continued, until tears and words were no longer. Loeric and Dileon refused to sleep and would only allow the girls to sleep when they were wrapped around a cloak with the men. They figured this would keep them warm enough to rest, and the men would be able to make sure they did not float off into a sleep of death.

Dileon struggled after three days to keep his eyes open. He began to see large deer walking in front of the small lean-to. His body was too numb to try and reach out to see if they were real or imagined. Loeric swore he had seen no game; if he had their bellies would already be full.

Trying to move enough to get more snow for water, the band suddenly heard the most terrifying noise of their lives. A whooshing noise was overwhelming overhead. When Loeric looked out over the lean-to, a dark winged bird with a metal body hoovered over the passage. A person was inside the bird! *How is this possible?* Loeric's brain tried everything to process what he was seeing.

This must be a magical dragon. Where is the fire? There is no fire coming out of its mouth! They eyes are clear as glass. This is no magical dragon. An even stronger sense of fear grabbled Loeric and his companions as his thoughts continued to wander in fear. *What dark magic is this? I must be hallucinating. The others must see it, they are looking at it. Surely, this cannot be our chariot to Valhalla.* The insides of Loeric's chest began to tighten as fear overtook rationality.

Confusion weaned as he realized maybe this bird thing could save them. Loeric moved the lean-to away from the small group. Snow fell and almost put the fire out. The girls were crying unable to bear the wind swooshing around their heads. The burning sensation on their faces made them blind to the helicopters approaching passengers. The young group had never experienced such an unknown situation.

The helicopter pilot had heard of a group of young kids traveling through the canyon alone. They had been spotted in the valley days before. When he went to assist the group and get them out before the snow began, the youth had disappeared. Now he knew why. He was startled when he thought he saw a small flame within the canyon passage.

Not being familiar with their surroundings; the group had no idea they were camping on top of a frozen river known to the locals as the *Snake River*. The helicopter piolet knew he needed to get these kids out immediately. The last storm of winter had finally passed, and Paul knew the weather would soon begin to warm up. In Wyoming, the weather was always changing. It would not take much for the ice to thaw out. He was amazed the group had been able to maintain a fire in the storm.

"Calling Teton tower, this is Papa Delta, over."

"Papa Delta we hear you, what's your request? Over."

"I have found the young group of kids we've been looking for. They look alive, but barely. Can you send a rescue team immediately? Over."

"We read you. I have a rescue team on standby. What's your coordinates Papa Delta? Over."

Paul relayed his current coordinates and then sat his helicopter down on top of the canyon walls. He had worked in these mountains for twenty years, and never seen such bravery or stupidity in the dead of winter. *These kids will be lucky if they make it out alive.*

It took twenty minutes, but the rescue team arrived and landed nearby Paul's aircraft. The team was made up of six local National Guard members who volunteered their time rescuing stranded hikers, hunters and any other brave souls looking to wander the Tetons unguided. The rescue team brainstormed a plan and then set it into action. Overall, from the first moment Paul spotted the group until the rescue was in action, only an hour had passed. This was a much-needed record if Anna, Zoey, Dileon and Loeric were going to survive.

****

Anna woke to the wonderful, familiar smell of her mother's biscuits and gravy. Anna loved biscuits and gravy. As she looked around Anna recognized her own things, but the room was not the small room of the apartment. Anna did not remember moving, *they must have moved during the short time I was in that place.* Anna found the large bathroom right next to her room and then proceeded into the kitchen.

It didn't take her long to realize it was a trailer home. The trailer was large and had two bedrooms. The second bedroom only had the single twin bed from the previous apartment. In the living room sat the cursed futon bed/couch. There was an entertainment center with a thirty-two-inch television sitting on top. *I wonder where that came from?* Anna was not much for television, except for when she was alone and then she would find some cartoons.

"Good morning sleepy head!"

"Hi mom."

Anna had so many questions for her mother but did not want to ruin the moment. For a little while Anna wanted to pretend her mother and she had this wonderful, perfect lifestyle. Anna looked out the kitchen windows. They were long, large, square windows. They did not quite reach the floor, but they were very open. Anna could see the neighborhood quite well. Rows and rows of trailer houses engulfed Anna's vison. *They had moved into the trashiest trailer park in all the town, state, and probably the worst one in the country!* Anna took a deep breath and reached up to give her mother a hug. Liz embraced her daughter and felt relieved to see Anna so happy and alert this morning. She knew Todd would be off work in less than an hour, and she should probably be home before then; but today Anna needed to spend a few minutes with her. Liz made a conscious decision to spend some extra time with Anna instead of rush home to Todd.

"Are you living here too mom?" Anna felt the answer in her heart before her mother answered.

"No. I am still at Todd's place. He misses you. He always says you are his favorite because you are so rebellious."

Anna's response was less than what Liz had expected it to be. "Can we just eat our food? I don't really want to talk about Todd or any other male person."

"I just wish you could be more underst-"

"Mom, please! Can we just have a normal breakfast?"

Liz did not want to ruin the moment either, so she silently agreed and continued to eat with her daughter. Finally, Anna broke the silence and asked the question most on her mind,

"When did we move here?"

"It was your coming home surprise. Rick felt like the apartment was too small, with only one bedroom and all. He got an advance and got this place. The rent is not much more than the apartment."

"It is nice to have my own room again. At least now I can listen to my music without worrying about waking up the land lady." Liz and Anna laughed. As they continued to finish their meal the girls talked about shallow topics and current gossip between all their friends.

Rick had left earlier that morning to go into work. He wanted to make sure Liz and Anna had plenty of mother-daughter time. He needed to play his part and play it correctly. Anna was old enough to marry him and he wanted to show her he could give her everything she wanted. The moment Liz left, Anna felt sad and lonely. She knew without her mother here there was no reason for Rick not to hurt her.

The school had been informed of Anna's hospital visit, and decided it was more than enough cause to drop her. Anna needed to figure out how she was going to finish school, escape Rick and still maintain her independence. Her mother and Rick already showed their hand. Anna knew they were now not afraid to lock her up and send her away. It scared Anna more than anything; losing her chance at freedom.

****

The rescue basket was not difficult to navigate going down. Coming back up, loaded with a passenger was a bit more difficult. The wind in the canyon was causing the rescue basket to swing back and forth. The pilot stayed as sturdy as he could while his crew worked the crane. One of the guard members went down into the basket to secure the passengers as they went up. Zoey was the first to enter the strange metal basket. When the man came down out of the metal bird with his strange armor, he was faced with four confused faces holding blades. Anna, Zoey, Dileon, and Loeric were freezing but were not going to die by the hand of a stranger while they were vulnerable.

"Woah…It's okay. I am here to rescue you. I am here to get you out of this death trap."

The teenagers looked at each other and put the blades away. "What is this strange contraption?" Anna figured she would at least try and figure out what magic was being used to rescue them.

"It is a helicopter. Have you never seen a helicopter before?" The young group each nodded in a confusing no. Anna was surprised as the man in the strange armor and clothing spoke to himself, she thought for a moment he was ready to curse them all.

"Mother Hen, I have a problem. There are two females approximately sixteen years old, and two males of the same age. Over."

"Baby bird, what seems to be the problem? Over."

"They are wearing mid-evil looking clothing and gear. I was greeted with broad swords. They have put them away, but I have a feeling they have no idea where or what time period they are in. We will need to radio ahead to call medical and have a team standing by. Over."

"Baby bird, we hear you. We will make necessary precautions. Can you start sending them up, I don't know how long I can hold her in place with this wind picking up. Over."

"Loading the first passenger now. Over."

"Who's going first?"

"In that thing?" Anna was stunned. She did not want to be hanging in the cold in the strange contraption.

Zoey spoke up immediately, "Is it warm up there?"

"Yes, we have blankets waiting for you." The man had been nice so far and Zoey figured if he was out to hurt them, he easily could have by now. She reached out as the guard member helped her into the basket. A moment later she was strapped in and being taken up. Zoey felt like she wanted to scream. She did not like the feeling her insides had while going upward. She could not see the bottom of the metal bird only an opening in the side of it. She realized she was going to have to climb into the bird from the side. She began to panic, but her body was so frozen she could barely breathe. Finally, she reached the helicopter as another strangely dressed man helped her into the hallow bird.

"You are okay. Hang on here. Okay now. Good job! You got this." Zoey could barely hear him over the sound of the helicopter blades. She climbed inside, and someone else grabbed her, wrapped her in something very warm and then placed a strange mask over her face and something over her hears. "Can you hear me better?" The man's voice came through the device over her ears. She shook her head up and down. The mask seemed to help her breathe a little better. She laid back in the seat, then one of the men strapped her in. She was afraid she was being taken prisoner, until one of them spoke to her again through the headphones. "It's to make sure you do not fall out." Zoey laid her head back and passed out.

It took another half hour to get the remainder of the group up to the helicopter. Once they watched Zoey make it up safely, the others were less hesitant. Dileon and Loeric insisted Anna go next, then each one followed. The guard noticed there was a cart and lots of supplies. "I don't think we can carry the supplies."

"It's okay. We do not have much left anyways. We only need our armor and our weapons."

"Can you tell me what you need, and I can send it up after you."

Loeric began to sort through the remaining supplies to find all he thought they would need. He used his last bit of strength to do so. His limbs were numb, and the cold steel stuck more than once to his fingers. Before he had a chance to go up in the basket Loeric blacked out from the cold.

"Mother Bird, last male, just blacked out. Stand by for emergency revival. Over."

"Standing by. Can you get him in the basket? Over."

"Yes. Sending him up now. Over."

Chris worked frantically and was able to secure the young man in the basket. He was strapped in on his back. Chris worked on covering his face and body as best he could. The wind was getting worse. He feared if they did not get out soon, the entire team would also be trapped. He watched the basket being lifted, another ten minutes passed, and it was brought down again. Chris loaded up the strange equipment, grabbed the top of the cables to the basket and signaled himself to be lifted.

"What is all of this?"

"The one who passed out insisted we bring their weapons."

"It's some shields and swords. This group is a strange one. The horses were frozen dead, and I do not believe anything else was salvageable."

"Interesting. Chris you always get the strange ones." Chris nodded in agreement while securing himself in the open passenger seat. The helicopter lifted straight up as George their pilot called in the emergency to the closest hospital;

St. Johns Medical Center. The flight took no more than ten minutes. Three of the four had passed out, and one of the young girls was on the verge of passing out. They used gurneys to escort each of the young people into the hospital.

Chris decided he would take the weapons back to the base with them. Later, after he wrapped and secured each piece, he could bring them back to the strange group. Chris did not want to see the group go crazy when they were confiscated by hospital staff. He was also looking for another reason to come back and figure out who these strange children were and why they were in the canyons. Chris felt something inside of him pulling at the group, his curiosity was not going to let this one rest.

****

When Tabitha had felt her magic begin to drain, she knew it was the end of her time in GothanVel. It was time for her to move forward. She never knew where she would end up or how she would appear, but the universe had an interesting way of putting her exactly where she needed to be. When she appeared in the new reality, she was surprised to find herself as a night nurse in a rehabilitation center. The first few days nothing unusual stuck out. Then on the third day, she noticed a familiar name; Anna.

Tabitha had much interest in this Anna. *Could it be? Has fate brought me to her?* She carefully read the file, as she became familiar with the strange girl, she decided it was time to go see for herself. She stood in the hallway looking in the window for several minutes. She was a mirror image, but she did not deserve to be restrained like that. Tabitha entered the room, but not before looking at her name tag to find out who she was; *Stacey R., R.N.*

*For what is reality but what we make of it?
God puts us where he wants us.*

*We can ask him to move mountains, and he will
provide us.*

*He placed us in those mountains for us to fulfill
his goals he already laid out for us.*

God knows yesterday, today and tomorrow.

Reality is now.

Chapter 1
Warmth

Warmth is found in the comfort of reassurances, not our fears where only cold lingers.

When Tabitha came into work the next night, she immediately went to see how Anna was adjusting to her new dorm. The long walk through the corridor was nothing new to the nurse who until recently had walked these halls for over twenty years. Stacey as she was now called existed only in the memories injected into Tabitha's memories. Stacey was the women who Tabitha's mind and spirit now occupied. Tabitha did not know exactly how the magic worked, but she knew only death would allow her to be brought to Stacey's body. If she had to guess, Stacey was dying or had just died when the magic took over. No lives were lost, that would not have been already lost. Tabitha's body in GothenVel had died and her spirit now occupied this body. Stacey's spirit was no longer here, only necessary memories needed for Tabitha to take over living her life. It was a difficult adjustment the first time it had ever occurred to

Tabitha but this being her third time making this type of exchange she was used to the process. The culture was an adjustment and having to learn at a very fast pace, otherwise the change was good.

When she died in the cave, she was not sure what fate would do with her next. Finding herself in the hospital working as a charge nurse for her granddaughter was a surprising shock. Tabitha was sure she would never have another opportunity to help Anna fulfill her destiny. What she did not know was whether a decision had been made yet. *She was in the other reality, but did this Anna know her destiny? Did she know what waited for her?* By the way Anna cried to her the previous night Tabitha suspected she did not. This Anna was in a hell of her own. Tabitha had to find a way to help her.

****

The cold had finally ended. Anna was warm. She never thought she could be warm ever again. The winter storm had been one Anna had never experienced in her entire life. *There must be some evil in this world for the weather to be*

*so terrible. In GothanVel when it snowed it was
a soft beautiful blanket of white. When it rained,
it came down hard, but refreshing. The storms I
have witnessed since coming to this strange land
scare me. What have I gotten us into?*

The incandescent lighting was unnatural to
Anna. This place she was in, it was too clean,
too white. The only assurance was the warmth
Anna felt in her body. Strange implements came
out of her arms and led to some type of clear
bladder holding liquids. She tried to remove the
object, but it would not budge. She looked at the
strange garb she was wearing. A small piece of
cloth tied around to her back and sides. The bed
she laid in was unlike any she had ever felt
before. It was not so soft it makes her sink, but it
was not too hard either. It was a weird sensation
under her body. Anna forced herself to sit up.
She looked around the room. She found there
were glass windows. *What is this place that they
can afford so much glass?* On the windows hung
strange colored drapes. They were cloth but
looked to be some type of lizard skin. Anna soon
found she was unable to move very far or the
object coming out of her arm; it began to pull

and hurt. Feeling awake, but thinking it a dream, Anna wanted her companions. She began to scream.

"Help me! Someone please tell me what is going on? Where am I? Where are my belongings?"

An instant later a stranger wearing long pants, and a weird tunic came in. She looked at Anna. She had a stern look and Anna settled immediately. Anna looked at the bracelet she found on her wrist. Jane Doe. D.O.B unknown. Approximately 16 years old. "Is this supposed to be my name? I can assure you my name is not Jane, and I am not a Doe."

The nurse paused her reading and looked at Anna for the first time. "What is your name then?"

"My name is Anna of GothanVel. Daughter of Eric. Can you please answer my questions? Where are my friends? My belongings? Where are we and who are you? Are we being held captive?"

The questioning look from the strange woman told Anna her words must have sounded strange. "My name is Terri, and I will be your nurse today. You are in a hospital; St. John's Medical Center. We have you and your friends in different rooms. Do you remember how you got here?"

Anna shook her head no. Suddenly, an image appeared in her head of a strange metal bird and the man named Chris taking her into the bird. "Actually yes, I remember being taken into the strange metal bird called a hell-i-opter?" Anna knew it did not sound right, but she hoped it was enough to satisfy this nurses questions. "We are not children; we do not need a nurse. We are capable of taking care of ourselves if you would please remove this contraption from my arm.'

Another confusing look came across the nurse's face. "I don't know where you come from, but here nurses and doctors treat all types of people, young and old. And here you are not considered an adult, but a teenage child. You cannot leave until we have contacted your parent or guardian. Do you know their names?"

"My parents died a long time ago, but my adopted father..." Anna hesitated, there would be no way Arvid would be able to save them from this strange land. "Well-we do not have parents in this world! I demand you release us immediately! I wish to see my sister and friends."

The nurse shook her head in disbelief, *did this girl just say this world? She just demanded we let them go? Where did this poor girl come from and what type of trauma has, she endured? It must be one of those cult villages. Chris did warn me, this was a strange bunch.* Terri hesitated and considered calling a psychologist from the psych ward to come and consult; for this child was surely in need of special care.

"Anna, as you say your name is. I cannot just let you go. I can however take you next door to see your sister. She has not woken up yet. We had to revive one of the young men you came with and he is currently in a coma- a deep sleep."

"Fine. Please take me to my sister." Anna was unsure about not asking about Loeric and

Dileon. As history had proven they often were able to handle themselves, so for the moment she left it be.

Against her best judgement, Terri reached over and carefully undid the IV Cord from Anna's arm. She replaced the needle with a band aid. She helped Anna out of the bed and insisted she sit in a wheelchair. Anna was intrigued by this wheeled chair. She did not hesitate and sat in the cold chair with the strange material; cold and rubbery, feeling much like the beaned chair they had summoned in the cave. A warm blanket was sat across Anna's lap and the nurse pushed her out the door and into the next room. Anna watched as Zoey looked to be in a peaceful sleep. Her face showed contentment. Zoey also had the strange contraption attached to her arm. She also saw a loud machine with wavy lines. "What is that!? Is it hurting her?"

"No, this is how we monitor her heartrate and oxygen levels."

Anna had no idea what the nurse was talking about. She just shook her head and moved in closer to her sister. Anna found Zoey's small hand, and gently placed her own inside her sisters. "Is she going to be okay?"

"Yes, she is only sleeping. You both suffered from hypothermia; and nearly froze to death. We are unsure how you even survived in such severe weather and circumstances."

Anna was familiar with hypothermia. It happened when someone fell in a lake at home during the cold months. She also knew it was a very serious and deadly illness. Tabitha, her grandmother, and clan healer had taught her immediate warmth and broth could help soothe symptoms but if a person developed a fever they could die. These strange machines must be what saved Anna and her friends.

Anna felt her sister move slightly. Zoey's head turned in her direction. "Anna? Is that you?" Zoey opened her eyes to see her adopted sister and best friend starring back at her.

"You are awake! Oh Zoe. We are in a terrible strange predicament." Anna turned to see the nurse still standing in the room, "DO you mind? My sister and I have much to discuss. We do not need an audience!" The nurse looked at Anna and huffed out into the hallway.

"Do you remember, before you disappeared, how we would go play in the flower fields?"

"Yes, of course! Those are some of my favorite and most cherished memories." Anna's eyes watered looking back and remembering the innocent play of the two girls in the long-ago memory. They seemed unafraid of anything. The girls never worried about potential harm or dangers, they just played. They enjoyed life.

"I miss those days and while you were away, I would yearn for them. I used to go by myself… well, until ma told me I had more important duties. I would pick flowers and offer them to Freya; an offering to bring you home." At this point even Zoey's eyes were filled to the brim with tears about to spill over.

"Zoey! I missed you so much! I have been so selfish; dragging you away and getting us almost killed. What was I thinking? I should have never pulled you away from home. When I was stranded-stuck in the woods, all I could think about was you, and wishing I was near you. Now that we are back together, I feel like I have mucked everything up."

"I chose to come along with you! There is no way I am ever losing you again sister. If it means traveling to strange lands and risking our lives than that is what I must do!"

"I have missed our long talks." Wanting to change the subject to something less serious Anna changed the subject. "Remember when we would giggle over Agnes tunic?" Agnes was the bitter old lady cook in the clan castle. She was a bossy one, but the girls still found ways to get in her away as she was constantly running the girls out of her kitchen.

Zoey giggled. "It would come out of her apron and look like she had a tail. I remember we used to joke and laugh and try to guess what kind of tail she had. Agnes would get so mad trying to get us to tell her what was so funny." The girl's laughter brought on stares from the nurses outside. They quieted down and although the laughter was a much-needed reprieve, they knew they had to discuss their present predicament.

Anna began to tell Zoey all she had discovered in the time she herself had been awake. "They will not release us, until we have parents or a guardian. We have neither. What will we do?"

Zoey knew they had risked a lot getting into the strange metal bird, but she also knew they were no longer lost in the snowstorm. They were warm and safe. "We are safe, and alive sister. What we must do now, is find food, I am much starved!"

Anna Laughed. She was the one that normally had an appetite like a horse. Today it was Zoey's turn to be the overly hungry one. After all they had been through who could blame her? Anna asked the nurses sitting in the center of an open room at a large desk area, how they went about getting food. The nurse brought them a large paper with many choices on it. Anna and Zoey had no idea what the choices meant. They could read the words, but had no understanding of their meanings?

"What is a cheeseburger?" Anna did not like the sound of onion rings either. She did however recognize the soup menu. Soups were very familiar in GothanVel and if it was something Anna and Zoey recognized it would probably do them good to have something soothing and warm in their bellies. They ordered enough for both as well as two extras for Dileon and Loeric. "Zoey, while we wait, I am going to go visit the boys."

After more confusing and frustrating information from the nurses, Anna finally convinced one to take her to her friends' rooms. Loeric looked in terrible shape. He had a strange tube coming out of his mouth attached to something around his neck. It looked as if a piece of cloth was suffocating him. Anna rushed to his side, and demanded a nurse remove the contraption before he choked to death. Thinking there was a true emergency the nurse ran in yelling *code blue*. When she saw Anna trying to remove the breathing tube, it panicked the nurse almost as much as a true *code blue*.

"What do you think you are doing? You cannot remove that!" The nurse was screaming at Anna and pushing her away.

"It's hurting him! Remove this contraption at once!" Anna felt overwhelmed and so lost. She did not understand any of these strange healing methods or ideas. The people here did not seem to be kind and gentle. All she wanted was to leave this place and go home. *Home.* The thought made her remember why she was in this strange land; *home was not her purpose. I must continue this strange journey in order to fulfill my destiny.* Anna slumped down in a chair next to Loeric and as her hands came to her face tears streamed down in an unexpected burst of emotions. Anna cried until she could cry no longer. The nurse finally gave up on lecturing her and stormed out. Before Anna could fully compose herself, the nurse returned with a doctor.

"The boy should be waking up any moment, so we might as well remove the tube. If he is anything like his friend here, he will try and remove it himself."

The doctor and the nurse removed the contraption around Loeric's neck and within a few minutes Loeric was breathing on his own and began to wake up. Anna still being upset and emotional was only heighted more at his eyes opening! While Zoey and Loeric were slowly eating soup, Anna was able to go see Dileon. He was in better shape and was so relieved and happy to see Anna. Sitting over the bed was a strange table covering half the bed.

"Anna! You are well! I was so worried about you!" Dileon jumped out of his bed, pushed the table aside, and as he neared Anna he picked her up into a large hug sweeping her off the ground. "Where are we? These people refuse to tell me anything."

"Something called a hospital. They say we cannot leave without a parent or a guardian. I do not understand exactly but I know we do not have any parents around. And we are Guardian's in our own rights. In this land one must be much older than myself to be called 'grown up'." Anna swung her head low and fought back the tears wanting to stream down her face.

"Anna, did you tell them how old each of us were?"

"No, only myself."

"Anna who do I talk to? I will get us out of here, just go along with me okay?"

Anna nodded in agreement. Dileon went outside and began to talk with the nurses. Unlike Anna and Zoey, Dileon was tall and able to look much more regale and more sophisticated than she ever remembered while they were in GothanVel. To Anna, they were all young children again, lost in a wild adventure. Seeing the way Dileon strode over to the nurses' station, made Anna realize she did not feel at all grown up.

"Greetings, my fair ladies!" Dileon used the traditional greeting of the GothenVel marketplace. He wanted to be as polite as possible. A traditional greeting would show respect and give a sense of trust while showing the women he meant no harm.

A few of the younger nurses began to giggle at the young man standing in front of them.

Dileon's look of happy and friendly, instantly turned into one of humiliation. *What did I do wrong to deserve such disrespect and humiliation? Do these women not have a customary courtesy?* Fortunately, even in this atmosphere, Julie had the respectfulness and professionalism to reply like a decent human being. "Hello. How can I help you?"

Hello. I can address this. Finally, something I understand. Although, not a greeting for strangers, but instead reserved for family, it works. The years of etiquette and training Dileon received did him little good in the world he now found himself in. regardless he was able to relax and repeat the greeting.

"Hello. My young cousin over there has informed me you are requiring of our parents or a guardian for us to leave this place. I believe you have been misinformed on our statuses, and of our proper titles."

Julie looked at the young man and tried not to stare or gap at his response. *Who the hell still talks like that? Maybe he is from one of those weird role play groups or something. Statuses*

and proper titles? Where are we; England?
"Young man. We require information on all minors; and a legal adult related to or in care of the minor must be present, otherwise we cannot allow you to leave. If something were to happen to you, we would be held liable."

"Let me assure you milady, Loeric and myself, were sent to escort Young Anna and Young Zoey on a much important and immediate mission. We are, as you stated, 'liable' for them. Their safety is our number one concern. As soon as you deem them well to travel again, we would be more than happy to sign any documentation required to see us off. We are their guardians!"

"How old are you? You cannot possible be the charge of these two young ladies!"

"I am twenty years old, and Loeric is also twenty. Just last moon cycle I believe. Their father Arvid left us to be responsible for their care and safety."

"Do you have any proof? Any paperwork stating what you claim, and what the hell is a moon cycle?"

Trying to stay as patient as possible, Dileon looked around to try and find something he could draw with to explain. After a few moments he noticed a square document hanging next to the desk. It looked to have little moons drawn on some of the squares. It was some sort of calendar. Different than the ones he was used to, but the same basic idea. He showed the nurse the different stages of the moon to the nurse and then realization hit her. *A moon cycle is one month.*

"Please milady. If you could get us started on any necessary documentation, we can be on our way."

"Your other friend-Loren or whatever you called him, cannot go anywhere. He practically died! The life flight team had to jump his heart to bring him back, and you want to just walk away and leave? Without proof of your guardianship or without the girls' father, I cannot just take your word for it. I would lose my job. Its not that complicated. Why don't you understand? Who are you people?" *Probably some type of cult that lives out in the middle of nowhere. One of those strange societies.*

Dileon was left just starring at the nurse. It seemed she wanted an adult to sign documents to release them but needed documents to show they were the adults that could do that. Dileon shook his head in defeat and headed back to where Loeric, Zoey and Anna waited patiently for his return.

****

The next shift Tabitha began to hear all sorts of gossip. The first bit of news surprised her. Somehow Anna of this world, had been released. The other news was even more shocking. A strange group of two girls and two young men had been admitted in the intensive care unit for hypothermia and after being warmed, fed and revived began throwing a fit about the care of the hospital; demanding to be released. Surprisingly, the girls called themselves Anna and Zoey! Tabitha had to sit down. She could not believe it! *Her Anna and Zoey? Here with her? But if the two Anna's met, what would happen? How could this be? Anna was supposed to choose her destiny How was this part of the plan?* None of it made any sense.

****

Anna filled out the paperwork. It took her nearly an hour. She had called her mother Liz to come down and sign it for her, she still needed an adult's signature. Considering Rick was the one who helped the secretaries drop Anna from school, she did not want to encourage any more participation on his part. She wanted to disconnect from HIM in any way possible. School was her place. It was all Anna had left.

After the paperwork was complete, Anna felt relief. She handed the paperwork over to the principal, Mr. Thomas. Supplies were not needed, as the school received grants allowing them to always provide what materials such as notebooks and pens the students needed. Anna still had her course books from before she was dropped from the roster. The principal had always been kind and helpful to Anna and was shocked when seeing Anna was dropped in the first place.

"Mrs. Bridges, why did it take you so long to let me know what happened?"

"I assumed you knew already. I didn't want to seem like I was making any excuses. The situation of me being in the hospital-well, it just sucked."

"When students are hospitalized, their placement at school is held indefinitely. Anna, this should have never happened. You are a good student."

Unsure of how to respond, Anna simply held her head low and mumbled a small thanks. She said her goodbyes and headed back to the place she was supposed to call home-the dreaded trailer park.

The quietness consumed the trailer house. Rick was working and Anna was enjoying as much peace as she could. Too afraid to call or visit friends, Anna decided to try and catch up on one of many books she had picked up during her last trip to the school library.

****

No matter how much Anna tried, she could not summon any magic from her stone or from anything around her. There was not enough magic in this world to help her. *What had happened to this world? Was there never any magic?* Tabitha had once told Anna that magic could disappear altogether if a society stopped believing in it. It would disappear and vanish into another reality. One that could use the magic. There were many aspects of Tabitha's teachings that made no sense. *I must be in another reality; the reality.* Tabitha said when I was in another reality, I would not be able to remember the other. She also told me my stone will give me what I need when I need it. If no magic works, her what was the purpose? Anna grasped the stone in her hand tighter. For a moment she thought it felt warm. Just as fast the cool sensation of the stone was all she could feel in her hand.

A lady called a *social worker* came to talk to Anna, Zoey, Loeric and Dileon. The story Loeric had told to the nurse the day before remained, but the social worker began to talk about moving Zoey and Anna to a 'group home.' Anna asked many questions but still could not understand 'the why' of the situation. She simply could not understand the ways of this strange world.

The social worker told Anna they simply could not confirm Loeric and Dileon's association and that it "was inappropriate" for two young girls to be with two older boys. She also explained to Anna if Loeric and Dileon oversaw the girls they could be charged with child endangerment because of where and how the four were rescued. Anna did not have a good feeling inside of her when talking to the social worker. She decided it would be best not to give her any more information. The way the social worker looked at the group said not only did the social worker not believe the group but that she was working against them, not with them. After the social worker left, a surprise visitor; the man who had rescued them came to surprise the small group.

Chris had delivered their weapons, wrapped and cleaned. "You must keep these wrapped up, and do not let anyone know what is inside, or they will be taken away. The workmanship is wonderful. These are relics."

"They are not relics, I made them less than two moon cycles ago!" Loeric felt a bit defensive hearing someone call his work old. He felt proud at the compliment, but someone needed to understand what was going on.

"I have been thinking a lot about where you were found. Can you please tell me how you got there? I promise I will not judge. I will listen not speak."

Anna gave the two young men and Zoey a questioning look but began as soon as they confirmed it was okay. So far what they had learned about this world was not good, and for the first time in their young lives they began to understand what mistrust truly was. No one here was loyal, they constantly heard nurses complaining to other nurses about each other, and then would do the same about the nurse they were complaining about to the nurse they confided in. It was a crazy cycle of lies and deceit. The young warriors did not understand this type of behavior.

Where they came from, the enemy was typically clearly defined. One knew who they could and could not trust and you never talked disloyal to anyone you worked with. They were your companions, your brothers and sisters. They were family.

This place reminded Anna of the story of creation. She thought about the god who disguised himself as a snake to trick the first man and woman. She felt surrounded by snakes; always hiding their true intentions.

Chris listened as Anna quietly explained their journey and what their purpose was. Anna even went on to explain that she had to learn what two realities she lived in. She believed this reality and the one she called home were the realities. She knew she had to choose her only one otherwise both would disappear. Chris understood some quantum physics, but even this was out of his league.

As he listened, he recalled a nurse in the Martin Rehabilitation building asking about a young girl named Anna Bridges, who had been admitted not that long ago. Chris had been escorting the young girl who had been life supported to St. Johns for a drug overdose into the rehabilitation facility. He wondered if the Anna, Stacey had mentioned had anything to do with this Anna and her friends. Was Anna Bridges the same Anna from GothenVel; just severally traumatized and unable to remember her life?

Trying to remember what the other young girl looked like it suddenly struck him; they looked exactly alike! Were they lost twins, but they had the same name? What was going on here? Anna kept explaining, but magic? Trans teleportation? This was all too unreal. Chris decided to contact Stacey and have her come talk to Anna. After permission from the group, Chris pulled out his cell phone and called the phone number for Martin Rehabilitation Center for Teenagers. He did not realize the stares from the young group, until after he had finished talking with Stacey.

The four looked at him, in wonder and amazement. "I have been trying to pull magic from this world but have been unable to. How did you communicate so quickly with no spells?"

It took a moment before he realized they had probably never seen a cell phone before. He explained what and how the cell phone worked. After being unable to convince them it was technology and science not magic, he gave up. Trying to explain what technology was led to trying to explain what science was. The only relation Anna and her companions could relate was spells, potions and magic.

By end of the conversation two hours had passed, Chris knew he needed to head out. His girlfriend was the jealous type and would not understand these young people at all. He promised he would not tell anyone their story and assured Anna no one would harm them. He just needed a few days to try and figure out how to help them. He would help them. Why or how Chris could not explain, but he knew he needed to help these young people find a way home.

He felt in his heart, mind and soul this was his purpose. Although, Chris still didn't believe in magic and kept convincing himself these kids were having some psychotic episode, he knew what he was doing was right.

Chapter 2

Re-connecting

The ones we love are only lost when we stop believing they are there.

The night had been peaceful. Anna was able to lay down in her soft bed with no disturbances. The book she was reading was about a young boy stuck in a dystopia world with no color. Everything was the same. She fell asleep imagining what it would be like. The dream was colorless except she found herself being stuck in a hospital room with no doors or windows, suffocating. She dreamt of dread. Anna quickly sat up, sweat pouring down her face. Her dreams were becoming incomprehensible to explain and made her wake panicky. Imaging Sean and Kaela, her younger siblings, playing peacefully helped Anna relax and fall back asleep.

This time no strange dreams came as the blackness of sleep came. The next morning, Anna woke up, showered, got dressed and headed for school. Thankfully, she still had her brother's car. It was an old car but got the job done. With the car, her life had become simpler;

she no longer had to take the MONSTER to work. There was no reason too. He had the old *Ford Tempo.* Knowing it was not the first day of school, Anna had to push down her butterflies. She didn't want to answer a million questions. She found a spot to park in the student parking lot, grabbed her backpack and headed inside.

A part of her felt strange as if everyone knew where she had been and what had happened. As far as Anna knew no one knew exactly what the story was. She didn't have any friends who sought out where she was or asked about why she had been gone. Her best friend Bobbie had been out of school for months now. When living in a life like Bobbie and Anna did, it was typical to miss so much school. That was the usual way Anna lived. She understood getting close to people only caused hurt and trouble. She longed for real friends, ones she could confide in and one's like on television where they were there for you no matter what. She knew her life was not a tv show. If it was, she would have been taken away and saved a long time ago.

The school Anna went to was considered an "alternative" high school. It was much smaller than other schools in the area and had much smaller classroom sizes. Unfortunately, the school had a reputation for being the school for "bad, or troubled" kids. To Anna everyone seemed pretty cool. There were no fights like at other schools, and kids just focused on getting their schoolwork done. Some drama occurred occasionally, but otherwise it was mostly just class work.

The best time of the day was before school; breakfast. For breakfast she could grab one of the delicious homemade large and chewy cinnamon rolls. Her favorite classes consisted of English, and art. Lunch was nice too. It was set in the middle of the school day unlike other schools that spread lunch periods out, everyone at this school had the same time for lunch. This was easy to do because the school maybe only had a hundred kids at most. The rest of the classes Anna just did her work and tried to stay focused. At lunch she could go to the park and read; it was nice to have an open campus.

Art class was relaxing because the teacher was like a combination of a flower child and a naturalist. She was firm but also very encouraging. It never mattered what Anna drew or did her art was encouraged. This was a much larger change from her junior high art teacher who always compared her work to her brother or other people. Ms. Ciamineo always appreciated Anna's work for what it was; her own creativity. Art helped Anna in many ways. It was a period during the day where she could relax and not think about the rest of her life. There were no thoughts of her mother, Todd, Rick, her father, or even worried about her siblings. Just art. It was peaceful and Ms. Ciamineo played calming music that helped.

English class was just as relaxing. Mrs. Oches was the nicest teacher Anna had ever had. She always encouraged Anna to read new books and worked very closely with each student to help them improve their writing and their overall skills in general. She wanted the best for every student. Anna never felt judged or misplaced in her class. These two teachers were the reason Anna kept going to school.

Mrs. Oches pulled Anna aside to ask her about her recent absences and where Anna had been. Anna felt no need to lie to her but didn't really want Mrs. Oches to worry about her either. "I had some medical complications that landed me in the hospital for a while." She felt bad about the omission of several details but knew Mrs. Oches wouldn't judge her and would understand. "I am just glad you are back at school. I want you to know I am always here for you if you need anything!"

"I know. Thank you. That means a lot." For some reason Anna always felt super emotional when people who truly cared reached out to her. How could she burden these people with the truth of her life? They did not deserve to be tormented by the monster or any other threat. Other than the encouragement and concern Anna could not think of a way Mrs. Oches could help without getting hurt herself. Anna knew she would just have to be strong enough on her own. How, she had no ideas or answers. She had made it this far; she would simply have to stay strong. If she died well the world probably would not even know she was gone.

****

Chris felt emotionally lost. Confusion and frustration overwhelmed his thoughts. "I must be going crazy." He wanted so badly to help these kids out. If even a month before he had found those kids in the mountains, he would have felt completely different. He would have blamed parents, or some other explanation on the appearance of those four kids.

A month before Chris had lost his younger brother to an accident in the mountains. Henry had been such a carefree teenager. He loved to hike the peak and continually challenged himself to be better, faster. Henry got caught in a midwinter snowstorm and lost contact with his climbing team. It bothered Chris to think Henry was out there somewhere on that mountain, alone, dead, frozen. Since Henry's disappearance Chris had begun to have diverse dreams. Henry would come to Chris and tell him he was better now. They would talk about their childhoods and things they wished they did better.

Chris knew Henry was gone forever. The dreams kept him clinging onto a false sense of hope. Then shortly before the group of four were found, Chris's dreams changed. He dreamt of four teenagers trapped on the mountainside. Instead of Henry stopping and talk to him Henry kept guiding Chris to help the youth. Until the day of the rescue Chris had no idea who these kids were, now he was getting ready to risk is life and career for the group. If he was honest with himself, it was a way to make up for not being able to say Henry. Chris felt Henry was guiding him to help.

He still did not understand what journey Anna and her friends were on or how he played into the scenario. The night before the helicopter medic spotted the children, he dreamt again of the four teenagers on the mountain. He somehow knew he would find these kids. He dreamt he would come across a young lady and her companions, but they were in strange clothing and needed his help. Every time in the dream he pulled away from the group in the helicopter he turned into a cliff and woke up. That night he dreamt repeatedly the only way to avoid exploding into the cliff face was to rescue the group. The next day when he guided the pilot to the mountain range, he was given surprised looks when they spotted the group. "How did you know they would be there?"

"I'm not really sure. Intuition, I guess." Unwilling to admit his dreams, Chris did not want to be the subject of mockery amongst his co-workers. Although, what he was planning he may as well have told the truth because his entire life was about to be scrutinized if he was caught for helping the same group of kids break out of the hospital. Some unknown force, he suspected Henry, continued to pull him towards the children. He had to help them. If he did not, he was afraid of the consequences of his dream.

****

"You mustn't argue with them. We have to find a way out of here. They say we are not prisoners, but they treat us as such." Anna's frustrations grew each day they were confined to the halls of this strange building. The healers, called nurses and doctors, were not nice and refused to answer any questions. At one-point

Anna had asked to speak to their leader and the nurse laughed at her. "Do you not have a leader? Are you the one in charge?"

Irritated the nurse just looked at Anna in disbelief. *How could one young girl be so demanding and annoying?* Julie had run every test and toxic screen test she could on the four teenagers. Not one had drugs or any unknown substances in their systems. Upon arriving at the hospital all four had been fingerprinted to try and be identified. The local police had just recently brought the results back to the nurse. Anna was Anna bridges a young local girl who had also been recently committed to the rehabilitation unit only weeks before. The strange thing was the timeline was interconnected. She apparently had been in two places at the same time. Julie knew that was not possible and assumed a clinical error had been made. The group of four had arrived during the time while Anna Bridges was still in the rehabilitation unit. The rehabilitation unit didn't discharge Anna Bridges until several days after this group had arrived. Surely there was a mistake somewhere. Either the fingerprints were mixed up, or someone misspelled a name. It happened all the time. The other youth were unknown. No fingerprint matches had been found and no missing persons matched the description of the ones called Zoey, Dileon or Loeric. It nagged at the back of her mind. Her job was not to care where this strange group came from only to treat them and get them discharged as soon as possible.

Zoey began to pace back and forth. "Anna have you been able to use any magic here?"

"No. Not even a small amount." Anna hung her head in defeat. "I even tried to summon a simple spell, but nothing occurred. My stone seems to be failing me."

"I do not understand why we were sent to this strange land if we are not even able to use the tools we were given."

"What about that healer-Stacey? She was very convincing about knowing our journey, our secrets and even claimed to be Tabitha! How is that possible?"

"I'm not sure Loeric. Somehow, I felt she was who she claimed to be. The only problem is we watched Tabitha fade away. Did we too, fade away, and this is some sort of hell or in between life? If so, we must have done something terrible wrong and have failed in our mission. But my grandmother told me if we failed something much darker would happen when two realities emerged!"

Dileon was not one to jump to conclusions. His battle strategic mind would not let him assume. He had to analyze and find the ultimate solution to the problem at hand. Arvid would never allow such callous assumptions to be made. He had to look at the most reasonable explanation to any situation. That is how their clan survived; thinking realistically and logically. Listening to Anna and Zoey's concerns he began for the first time in his life to doubt his decisions. *Had they strayed from the mission?*

"We should try and get out of this place and continue on. To where…I do not know. Arvid would not want us just sitting here!" Dileon knew he had to protect Anna at all costs;

he refused to lose her again. He loved her too much.

"I have not had a true vision since we have been here, and Anna has been unable to use her magic. She wasn't even able to heal Loeric!"

"Has anyone checked the map?"

All eyes turned to Dileon. They had forgotten about the ever-changing map. The map that lead them to their current predicament. Surely, it wouldn't work in a world without magic. But if there was no magic how were they able to transfer to this strange land? So many questions and not enough answers.

"I had the map with me when we were taken up into the metal bird. I think it's in my belongings over there." Loeric pointed to an unusual white bag with hard plastic handles. Anna opened the bag and found the map rolled up alongside his other belongings.

"At least they did not take this from us."

The map no longer showed the endless expanse of mountain range like it had before. It had seemed a lost guide when the group made their makeshift camp in the devastating storm. The map also did not simmer as before, but instead showed a grid with many buildings and names of streets everywhere. A small falcon was lit up in a building called St. John's Hospital.

"This must be where we are! I think the map still works!" Berating herself for not remembering the map sooner, Anna's excitement grew as they now had a sense of renewed hope. Between Tabitha…well Stacey, as she was now called, Chris the man who had saved them, and the hope of the map still working they could likely get out of this strange land and go back to where they belonged. But what about the mission? Could Anna choose to go back home and risk everyone in this reality dying, or chose to stay in this strange reality? Tabitha taught her when the time came, she would know the right path. She had to choose. The sacrifice of her own life, for all of those she loved. Would she have to sacrifice her life? If so, she was willing. This unknown reality did not seem to like them, so she would have to choose the one that did. Anna made her choice. She chose, home. She chose GothanVel.

Something inside of Anna ate at her. She had made the choice, but nothing was changing. *Of course, it is not that simple. There must be more. But what?*

Chapter 3

Abandoned

In moving forward the gravel is steep; the terrain is uneasy, and the roads are tangled. To go up, one must go down, to go down, one must go up. No one unseen travels far.

"Please, I don't know what you want from me! Haven't I done everything? Haven't I been good? I need you to let me go!" Anna struggled to sleep peacefully. When she finally did go to sleep Anna was woken up again by HIM. HE could never let her rest or dream for long. It began to show in her schoolwork, on her body and in her head. Reality was becoming a thin line. She could barely eat, and when she was able to hold down a full meal, she felt sick.

It had been a month since Anna left the Rehabilitation Center. Only one person had called to "follow up" with her. It was the night nurse Tabitha, who had listened to her and allowed her to cry on her shoulder. The one person she had opened-up to in years. When she had called, HE had been right there listening to every word. As soon as the phone hang up, Rick began yelling at her.

"What did you tell her? I knew you couldn't keep your little bitch mouth closed!" Rick was furious. He wasn't going back to prison. *Why couldn't he just go find some whore to fuck, like everyone else? No, he had to have this girl. This young, sweet girl.*

Lately, this girl was becoming more a pain in his ass. He was making good progress before her stupid mother showed up that night. Ever since, Liz had been calling daily to make sure everything was going well. Of course, Rick would lie to her and tell her everything she wanted to hear. Anna was too scared to do anything but agree with the lies. Now it was time to make this little girl listen again. Each night was a fight to redeem his control over her. She was getting useless.

"I never wanted to be here! I don't want to be here anymore! I am never going to marry you; I will NEVER be Yours!"

Anna knew the moment the words came out of her mouth she would regret them. A fist came flying at her face. She went to duck as the blow struck the back of her head. As Anna was thrown down on the carpet of the trailer living room, she wanted to cry out, scream anything, but no scream would escape her lips. Rick Pulled off his belt rolled Anna onto her back. Anna refused to move, but he was more powerful. The belt stung the back of her butt as he whipped her repeatedly. After a few minutes Rick stopped. He was wearing out, too tired. *I'm getting too old for this shit.*

Anna was still on her stomach facing down on the carpet. "I know what I'll do with you. If you won't listen like a good girl and want to act like a ravaged animal, I will treat you like one."   Anna had no idea what he had conquered up now. *Hasn't he already taken everything away from me. What's the worst he can do? Kill me?* Rick pulled Anna's pants off her and threw them aside. He then pulled her shirt off, but Anna was simply limp and numb. She didn't care anymore. Rick continued until the young girl was completely naked. He bent her over the futon bars and had his way with her, not the usual way but what every animal deserves up her buttocks. *This will show you!*

The pain Anna felt made her want to scream out and fight, but she still could not. Her body took the abuse, as it just laid there. Anna could feel Rick completing his business, but as usual he was not happy. He seemed more upset. The trailer house faced other trailer houses on the front side. The back of the trailer house faced a small hill with miles of open land behind it. Unless, someone was exploring the back yard or coming from the open land it was hard to see anything in the back yard from the street. Rick threw Anna over his shoulder; he avoided the blood running down her legs and took her out the back door. An old dog leash and chain had been left attached to the back porch; left by the previous tenants. Rick undid the collar and attached it to Anna's neck. "Stay! Don't you dare try to come back in this house until you are ready to be a good pet." Rick walked back inside and closed the door.

The snow had padded most of the ground when Rick dropped Anna. The cold outside was bitter and was seeping into her skin. Anna just sat numbly as she hoped the cold would take her away. Naked, alone, abandoned. Anna had stopped wondering what she had done so wrong to deserve such a cruel life. At this cruel realization she stopped trying to think at all. *Lord please end this. Take me away.*

****

Chris looked at his watch. After a month of planning, he was ready. Chris used every connection he had established over the years to keep the young kids in the hospital together. He even had a psychiatric doctor friend of his analyze their 'combined trauma' as a necessary reason to keep the youth at the hospital and out of a group home. His hope was the psychologist would diagnose the group with psychotic disillusions. It worked for the time being. If the kids were in the hospital, they were helpable. If they got lost in the system Chris would have a more difficult time saving them; helping them.

Chris' jealous girlfriend had left him and moved out of his apartment yelling that he had lost his damn mind and was obsessive with work and teenagers he barely knew.   Chris had refused to give Carmen any information and the only information she could gather was through overhearing phone calls with Stacey.

Stacey had been a saving grace through all the planning. She gave Chris information and help where he was unable to find it. Never believing in anything other than science, Chris found even himself baffled by the four teenager's story. Even more he found Stacey's story even odder. He believed them. If someone were to ask him why, there was no logical explanation. He simply felt the same inner pulling inside him to help them. It must be his destiny. Since he had finally embraced the idea, he no longer dreamt of his deceased brother Henry or suffered from nightmares.

****

Stacey learned quickly who to trust and who not to trust. She even convinced her boss to let her move over to the long-term care unit so she could be closer to Anna, Zoey, Dileon and Loeric. Stacey knew it was an adjustment trying to figure out this new reality. This new world. She had explained to Anna during their training in GothenVel that there was only one world with multiple realities, but she believed this was truly a different world. Nothing was the same. Cars, trucks, planes, and helicopters! Machines that made things for you and could heal you? Lights and electricity? This world did not have the same magic as where Tabitha and the children came from, but it did contain its own magic; technology.

"How are you all doing today?"

Stacey entered with a few bags of food from a local fast food restaurant. She had been exploring many of the food options and shared them with the youngsters.

"I brought you something called Chicken nuggets. They are not droppings of chickens but fried chicken pieces, they even have a sauce."

The young group seemed to be catching on quite quickly. Another nurse that Stacey had learned to trust had gone through her grown children's left behind clothing and had been able to bring the youth some normal clothes to wear. Anna was not too happy at first, but after a few days she adjusted and liked the soft fabrics.

Zoey, always the fashionista loved the different styles once she figured them out. She enjoyed the bra the most. Dileon and Loeric adjusted easily as well, taking notice of the small differences in the pants and tunics, but noting they were not much different than what they were used to wearing. Underwear for the young men was an adjustment.

"You have to wear it, otherwise the rough fabric of the breeches will hurt you."

"It seems so tight. I just do not feel right." Loeric was always complaining about the new under clothes.

"Eat up. We don't have much time."

Stacey wanted to make sure the youth had regained strength enough to leave this place. She had been outside, and it was a confusing, large civilization. There were more people in one place than Stacey had even seen in her entire existence.

"Today is the day. Chris and I have been planning your escape for quite some time now. There is no time left. At 5 pm; when the moon begins to come out and the sun goes down, a social worker is coming to pick each of you up. Anna and Zoey, you are going to be put into a girl's home, and Loeric and Dileon you will be taken to a boy's home. The psychologist came to the conclusion you were closer to 16 and not 20; unfortunately, he saw through your story. There is less chance of escape or finding each other again if this happens."

Each person shook their heads in understanding. If this was going to happen, it had to happen now.

"Chris will be showing up with papers in just under an hour, stating you must be released to him, that he is the one to transport you."

"Will they believe him?"

"Yes, until the social worker comes to get you. When they come and find out someone else has already taken you, they will know what we did. The people here are ignorant and believe almost anything they are told. Just act as if you are disappointed but move quickly. I will then be waiting outside in the car."   "What is a car again?" Zoey knew this had been explained to her, but she was having a difficult time understanding how it was possible. A moving carriage without horses seemed a bit much. Even after her helicopter experience and looking out the windows to see the strange moving machines she still was not sure she could grasp the concept.

"Zoey, I do not have time to explain it again. Trust me. Eat quickly and grab your belongings. It won't be long now."

Stacey left to wait for the call letting her know Chris was there. As he came to the unit, Stacey would be leaving to get the car out front. Driving was a bit of an adventure until she practiced a few times. The memories flew into hers as if she had not missed a day driving in her life. It came so naturally to her now. The van they had rented only had two back seats but would be large enough for all six of them. Seven when they found this world's Anna.

****

It seemed like days. Anna knew she had only been outside a little while. The cold made her sleepy. More than once she had closed her eyes and leaned up against the wooden stairs. At one point, she climbed under the porch to avoid the cold air. The chain around her neck pulled her hair and didn't allow her to lay down. She was forced back out of the porch. Not long after initially throwing her outside and placing the collar on her, Rick had returned with a small lock. Momentarily, he had taken it off the freezing girl, only to pierce a small hole in the collar. He replaced it on Anna's neck with a small lock attached. It made it heavy around her neck.

"Let me come inside. I will do whatever you want. Please- Don't make me stay out here."

"Animals stay outside. Only good pets get to come inside."

It had taken all her energy to plea for warmth. Rick was more than a monster now; he was death itself. More long minutes passed, and Rick threw a blanket out the door. The slamming of the door made Anna look up. She could see the blanket a few feet away. Crawling through the cold snow she was able to barely reach it. Reach it she finally did, and she could feel the little bit of warmth remaining from being inside the house. Bundling the small blanket around the top of her she was grateful for the small comfort.

Not knowing exactly Rick had set out a bowl of water and another of some mushed up something. She had thought she heard his car start up earlier but, in the cold, she had thought she seen a lot of things. Going up to the porch she was not able to reach the top of the stairs but was able to reach for the bowl of water. She drank what little there was and grabbed the other bowl. She couldn't believe it. He had put dog food in the bowl for her eat. She sat the bowl back down. *She would starve and freeze to death before she ate that.*

****

The papers were not hard to forge. The difficult part was getting a seal to stamp the papers with. The official documents had to be stamped with the Clerk of District Courts seal otherwise it would be pointless. Stacey had watched many people show up with stamped paperwork and the nurses wouldn't even look at the rest. The seal was what was important. The information in the paperwork looked real enough.

Chris had a friend who worked in the office at the courthouse and once in a while he took his friend energy drinks and snacks. A week before Chris finally found an excuse to visit his friend. While distracted Chris pulled the stamp away from the desk and pocketed it. His heart almost stopped beating as his friend thinly missed his theft.

"Where did that damn thing go now?" Agitated his friend walked over to a drawer and grabbed another stamp. "These things go missing all the time! Someone's always too lazy to go get their own and steal mine!"

Chris shrugged, said his farewells and left to complete the planning.

Stacey waited nervously, until Chris finally called. "We're a go. Is everything ready?"

"Yes. I was even able to get the address of the other Anna. We must gather her too."

"I know. I will be there shortly. Be ready to go."

"I will. So, will they."

As Chris hung up the phone, his nerves began to turn to jelly. *Would this work. What was he doing? This was kidnapping, or at least making him an accessory to a criminal act.* As his mind raced, he calmed himself and focused on the task at hand. Freeing these young kids, from a hospital meant to save lives. In some ways he wondered if it would just be better to let things take course. Let the young troubled kids go into homes and get the treatment they needed. The other part of Chris told him it was all wrong. There was something much larger than himself at work here.

Pulling up to the hospital, Chris gathered his ID badge and the forged paperwork. He walked into the hospital and rode up the elevator to the pediatric unit. The nurse didn't even look at the paperwork. Just accepted it and handed it back to him. Chris signed a clipboard, with a fake name, and waited as the four teenagers were brought out to him.

*****

A few days prior, Stacey had asked a nursing assistant on the floor how to find information for a follow up call on a patient. Conveniently enough the assistant typed in the name and pulled up an address and all the information Stacey needed without question. Stacey printed off the information and tucked it away in her scrub pocket. Waiting anxiously the time seemed to slow down. Tabitha had much practice waiting. She had spent entire lifetimes waiting for new adventures and magical concepts to transform and take place in her life. This life was nothing new, but today she knew the fate of everyone could be in the hands of her.

Zoey, Loeric, Dileon and Anna walked swiftly but quickly to the van Chris led them too. Chris had told them to follow him and to act as if they had done this a million times. Walking out of the hospital was nerve wrecking and eventually when the elevators opened into the parking garage Chris was able to take a deep breath. Being too afraid to ask questions the group left the hospital and ventured out into the crazy world once again.

Anna stared at the map watching the falcon follow their every move. She was amazed to see some type of magic if only she could access it for herself. What seemed like ages, and many stops later, the group began to drive towards the end of town. Stacey had driven the day before to find the address of this worlds Anna. It had taken about a half hour to drive across town but eventually she had found it. As they approached the address, another vehicle pulled into the driveway. A man about 5 ft 8 stepped out of a small blue Ford Tempo. He had a rough beard and wore a blue work shirt and grease covered jeans. Anna began to feel a sense of evil coming from this man. "Why are we here?"

Stacey had not yet told them of her plans to gather both Anna's together. The group had assumed they would hide out in a safer shelter and come up with a plan to escape this strange world. Now, they seemed in a place of wooden and metal boxes that housed people, but it felt odd, off. Anna did not like the feelings she was receiving. Even Loeric and Dileon were nervous. Dileon had unwrapped his sword and had it sitting facing downward as if he was ready to get out and fight. The group sat in the van and watched the strange man go into the house and walk back out again.

Rick was tired, exhausted. All he could think about all day was coming home to a dead girl. He would then have to bury the girl deep enough so no one would ever find her. *The blanket will have helped her. I cannot deal with her fighting me. I want her to be good and listen. Why can't she understand that? She is mine. Given to me.* As Rick's thoughts went into circles, he was too occupied to notice the van sitting across the street watching him. He stepped off the porch and went to his Brighteyes. She was not dead. She was very cold, but not dead. He slapped her face, to bring her attention to him. With her head held low, he brought her eyes to meet his. Anna kept her eyes turned downward. She felt defeated. She just wanted to die.

Stacey and Chris noticed the girl first. A deep intake of breath did not help the anger Chris felt build up in his chest. He could not see the entirety of the girl but could tell she was huddled against the porch on the ground. Thinking about whether to storm over and face the man or wait it out to see what happened Chris and Stacey held each other back.

"Are you ready to be a good girl?"

Anna could barely nod her head but nod she did. As much as she felt she wanted to die, hunger and cold ate at her. Her fingers were blue and black as were her toes and she could no longer feel her legs. As if Rick was not the one to put her in this situation in the first place, he gently undid the lock and collar and lifted Anna up into his arms.

"It's all going to be okay Brighteyes, I will take care of you. Don't you worry now."

He carried her inside and placed her into the bathtub. He began to run a lukewarm bath. The pins and needles Anna felt against her skin made her want to scream. She no longer had a voice. The scream never left her head. As the water began to get warmer, she let it soak into her filthy body. Rick drained the water several times and each time filled the tub up with warmer water. He ran his hand over her forehead

as a father would comforting a child. Anna was
too lost to care.

"We cannot be naughty; you will behave
and listen to me." Another nod.

Rick took a washcloth and ran it up and
down Anna's body. It was a sensual motion that
sent a strange warmth over her. He massaged
every curve, every inch, she began to feel alive
again, until THE MONSTER came back out.

Stacey and Chris discussed with the group
who was in this place and why they were there.
"We need to get the girl. She is part of your
destinies. I was not aware of another person
being so close to her."

"Was that the girl we seen being carried
in?"

"I am afraid so Zoey."

"What are we going to do?"

"How can we help her?"

"We are going to go get some food and
some extra supplies, like clothing and blankets
and then we are going to come save her."

No one in the group understood exactly what needed to be done or how to help the helpless girl, but they felt and knew it had to be done. It was time to embrace the destiny. It was time to choose.

Chapter Four

Revival

From death there is a light of hope in which we are reborn. From life there is a sense of death. Do not embrace either for a destiny is only accomplished through blind faith of neither life nor death.

The town was another half hour away but the group of five needed a place where no one would be looking for them. A small restaurant served as a stopping point for the tired travelers. Anna could not get the girl out of her mind. *Who was this strange girl? Why did I feel so attached to her? I understand the cold she suffered, how long was she outside?* Many questions remained in everyone's minds until the food arrived at the tables. Anna liked a restaurant. It was very similar to the way food was served at home. The difference was you got to pick what food you wanted. The menu was simple and easy to interpret. With Stacey and Chris's help the four teenagers found something satisfying to eat.

"A roast is meat with potatoes and other vegetables?"

"Yes." Chris still did not understand exactly where this group had come from. Never believing in magical world or different realities he struggled to comprehend why they did not understand everyday concepts such as what a roast was.

"I think I will have the Roast!"

"Me too!" Dileon did not have the energy to look over all that was offered as he had thoughts of the young girl being carried into the 'home' as Stacey had called it. He knew he needed his strength, but his objective was to protect Zoey and Anna. This other girl was getting in the way of that.

The girls decided on a meal called chicken dumplings over mashed potatoes. Anna was more excited to see what mashed potatoes were that the actual meal itself.

"I have never mashed a potato before! I have eaten whole potatoes; I have eaten cut up potatoes, but I have never eaten mashed potatoes."

Stacey laughed as her granddaughter took in the simplicity of food. This new world felt familiar to Tabitha yet, so distant. Had she been here before, she was sure of it. Not in her current lifetime but another. When this journey began Tabitha did not foresee her full role in Anna's destiny. She knew Zoey, Loeric and Dileon would go home. They would live their lives as if nothing had really happened. They may not even remember this strange land or the events taking place now. They were here to help Anna. To save Anna. This Anna did not need help. Tabitha knew the Anna of this world did. What help was needed she could not understand yet. She was afraid. *Who was that man? How did he play a role in everything?*

******

Rick took every advantage having his Brighteyes warm up in the tub. He pleasured her with his hands and made soothing comments about how beautiful she was. He didn't care she was broken; all he could see what a beautiful girl that belonged to him. He drained the bathtub and grabbed a towel. As he lifted his prize out of the tub, he had a moment of weakness wanting to take her right then and there. But she was no good to him almost lifeless. Her eyes were closed but she was not sleeping. She was exhausted. She took her into the room and shut the door.

Anna didn't want to move. She laid on the bed for a few minutes before starting to get cold again. She never wanted to feel that kind of cold ever. She sat herself up and moved to the small dresser and closet where she kept her clothes. Anna did not want to be thrown outside again and knew in order to save herself she would do whatever HE wanted her to do. She found a pair of long thigh high stockings and a warm winter dress that went to her knees. Anna put on a bra and panties and made her way out into the living room where HE waited for her.

"Come, sit down." Anna did what she was told to do.

"I'm going to brush your beautiful hair." Anna sat down on the floor and crossed her legs.

"No, I want you to sit with your legs up." Anna adjusted herself so her legs were bend in a triangle forcing her to lean back against Rick. "Good Girl that's my Brighteyes."

Rick kept his tone soothing and calm. As he brushed her hair with one hand his other would explore around her face and throat. If Anna pulled away from the brush, he would gently grab her neck and pull her back towards him. "All done. Now what should we do? Are you hungry? I have food for my Brighteyes." Anna nodded. She was too afraid to say anything. Fear made her words stay frozen. Rick came back and sat behind her on the couch once again. In his hands he had a bowl and a plate. The plate had a square pizza he had made in the oven. Anna could smell the deliciousness of it. The bowl she could see or tell what was in it.

"You have been a very good girl Brighteyes, but you were still a very bad girl before weren't' you?" Anna nodded.

"Bad girls don't get what everyone gets. I made you some fresh food, but you have to eat it

all, and maybe I will share my pizza with you.
Do you understand?" Another nod.

Ricked placed a spoon into the bowl and
told anna to turn around and open her mouth.
Like a small baby he made her open her mouth
and take in the spoonful of mush. Anna couldn't
process what it was it was some type of meat
mixture. It made her gag reflexes react.

"Don't you dare spit that back up or I will
make you go back outside!"

Anna swallowed the food. Each bite given
to her was followed by Rick eating a piece of his
food. The smell of the pizza tortured Anna's
mind. She began pretending the food being force
fed to her was the same pizza being used against
her. Eventually, all the food was gone, and Anna
was told to face the other way. Her stomach
ached from too much at once, and she felt the ill
taste of the food in her mouth. At the same time,
she felt the hunger reside and go away.
Whatever he had fed her, at least it was
something to sustain her. Through feeling sick,
Anna began to feel some small sense of strength
return to her.

****

After the restaurant the small group went to a motel. The motel had two large beds, a bathroom off to the side, a television and a small refrigerator and microwave. After everyone was settled into a comfortable spot the group began making plans on how to get the girl.

*****

For what seemed like hours the television showed women pleasing other women. Men having sex with women, men pleasing men and all other types of pornography. Rick would force Anna's head back to the television whenever she looked away.

"Do you see how they do that?" Rick would continually comment on different positions and actions taken by the men and women on the screen.

"I want you to do that to me Brighteyes. Wouldn't that feel so good?"

Eventually, the television was shut off and Anna was told to stay as if she were a dog. Rick came back in nothing but shorts. He sat in front of Anna as he held the much-dreaded syringe that landed her in the hospital only a short while before. Rick tied her arm off with the blue band and held her arm out while he inserted the liquid into her veins. A short while later Anna's mind and body began to betray her. The feeling of wetness between her legs and pleasure throughout her body Anna knew she was in trouble. The MONSTER began.

Chapter 5

The Rescue

Not knowing all the ways of this strange new world. The small group came up with a plan. It took the help of a picture box called a television, but they were also battle tested youth. They would knock on the door and pretend to be new neighbors wanting to say hello. If that man answered they would bust their way in and take the girl. If the man did not answer they would break in and take the girl. Tabitha would provide the transportation and then they would work on getting back to their own time. If they could save the girl, then maybe all would not be lost.

Anna had much to contemplate. She still had to choose. This girl: this Anna that was like her was battling life in such an unimaginable way. Didn't she deserve to live a good life too? Maybe once they saved her, she could finally decide.

After bathing in a tub, and everyone eating, get cleaned up and preparing for the next day, the small band of youthful warriors closed their eyes and prepared for the battle ahead.

Anna was sore. She was scared but had resolved herself to being happy that she was inside and warm. No longer on the cold ground she was able to wrap the warm blanket around her body. The collar was still attached, but the Monster who controlled it was no where around. Anna forced herself up into a sitting position and crawled her way into the shower. HE must be at work. At least, God had provided me with some small blessings.

Anna could not stand awfully long so she settled on a bath. The water burned and stung every part of her body, but she knew she needed to get cleaned up. At any time, HE could return and who knew what new Hell awaited her. The night before she had been treated worst than a dog. Things had been done she couldn't even wrap her mind around. She wanted nothing more than to wake up from this prison. To be free.

At some point Anna must have fallen asleep. She was awakened by the sound of a knock on the door. She was not able to move fast enough. Anna grabbed her towel and started to get out of the bath. Wobbling she slipped; all Anna could see was the blackness surrounding her eyes.

****

Loeric kicked down the door, and Anna, Tabitha and Dileon followed Loeric into the strange box house. It was quiet until they heard the sound of a large object or someone hitting the ground. They ran towards the sound.

"Everyone get back, she has slipped and knocked herself out!" Tabitha immediately began taking steps to help the young girl. Beside the bath their sat a strange thick necklace with metal tags on it. A large padlock hung from the necklace. "What madness is this?" This must have been what was holding the poor girl to the ground yesterday! Tabitha picked Anna up and moved her into the closest room. There were scars and bruises all over the poor girl's body. Anna of GothanVel found some clothing and helped Tabitha cover the poor girl up. There was no blood and the Anna of Earth was starting to come too.

"Where am I? Who are you?"

"We are here to help child. Just relax this will all be over soon."

The band of warriors carried Anna to the vehicle and began to drive out of town. The further they got her away, the better her chances of survival were. None of the group looked out of place, and everyone seemed to be more relaxed. Anna of GothanVel knew what she had to do. She had made her choice.

She chose to give the other Anna life. She knew she would be gone forever but it was the obvious choice. Anna would no longer be selfish, and she felt her journey was complete. She had saved this girl from a horrible creature and the time for her was over. It was time to make everything right again.

The travelers came into a small town and followed the signs to the local hospital. Tabitha took Anna in and made sure the nurses and staff knew what the poor girl had been through. As soon as she returned to the SUV, Anna confessed to Tabitha her choice and why she had made it.

"I know child. The choice was yours, but it was already made a long time ago. I am so glad you have decided not to fight it."

Within minutes of Anna's confession, the world began to blur. Anna screamed as she watched her childhood friends fade from her vision. Everything became dark and swirled around her.

*****

"Code Blue! Code Blue!" The doctors ran into the hospital room where the young victim of violence started to crash. Her vitals had flatlined and the doctors screamed for the crash cart. It only took a few minutes, but Anna of the Earth began to level out. Her vitals stabilized and she was finally starting to recover from her horrible ordeal. The staff after meeting the strange nurse, made the girl a Jane Doe and had called the police. The nurse that dropped the girl off gave the address of the man who had done this to her. Nancy, the head nurse had kept in contact with the police of the town and found out, they had arrested the man on charges of drugs, sexual assault, and unlawful imprisonment of a person. Nancy did not know what this poor girl had been through, but she would make sure she never had to go through anything like this again. She hoped the man named Rick was locked up and put away for a long time. The police officer had told Nancy they had enough evidence to convict for a life sentence. The girl would never even need to testify.

The lady named Tabitha had never called to check up on the girl and no one seemed to know who she was, just a mysterious angel. Nancy had experienced much weirder in her twenty years as a head nurse.

"She's awake." Nancy ran into the room.

"Hello there! Do you know where you are?"

"No…I feel really woozy."

"Its just the medicines. It will ware off shortly. I'm Nancy. Your safe now. No one will ever hurt you again."

Epilogue

Anna spent months in the hospital and in rehabilitation programs. She was seen by counselors and doctors and many different nurses. Nancy always checked up on Anna and helped her in any way possible. Anna eventually, physically recovered. The internal scars would stay with her forever. Anna fought the courts and won independence from her parents. She became an emancipated minor. She was able to get a job, and a new apartment where she only had to deal with herself and her nightmares. Even the nightmares began to fade away. Eventually, Anna married a wonderful man named John and had three wonderful children. They moved out of state and began a new life in Iowa. Anna never had to look back at the nightmares she faced as a child. Her life was complete.

The only question was who had saved her, and where were they? According to the doctors and nurses Anna had been in a coma for quite some time. She never left the hospital and had never been admitted before that night. All the events she experienced where thought to be in her head. For Anna, they were real. The people who saved her from that nightmare. Where did they go? The girl just like her? The grandmother? The friends? They had to be real.

No matter the distance Anna found herself with her past, these questions always lingered in her mind. She often had dreams of strange lands and mysterious people, but the dreams never came to fruition. All that had really mattered was Anna had been saved with much gathered strength by her own Knights.